My Five Senses

by Mary Atkinson
photographed by Daniel St. John

I have two eyes.
I use my eyes
to see.

I see flowers
in the park.
The flowers look pretty.

I have two ears.
I use my ears
to hear.

I hear a bird
in the park.
The bird sings a song.

I have a nose.
I use my nose
to smell.

I smell food
in the park.
The food smells good.

I have a mouth.
I use my mouth
to taste.

I taste ice cream
in the park.
The ice cream
tastes sweet.

I have two hands.
I use my hands
to touch.

I touch the dog
in the park.
The dog feels soft.

see

smell

taste

hear

touch

13

I can use all my senses at the park!

The Five Senses

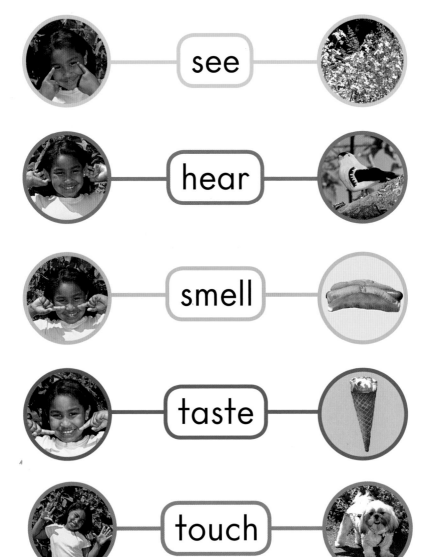

see

hear

smell

taste

touch